Observers *8*

**European Australian observations
on Chinese Australians**

**From the "Piece of *8*" series of
Chinese Australian History
in 88 Objects**

by

Michael Williams

Observers 8 - European Australian observations on Chinese Australians

First edition. October 1, 2024.
Copyright © 2024 Michael Williams.

ISBN: 978-1-7635605-4-3
Written by Michael Williams.

Published by: Chidestudy Press
For inquires or to order copies
Email: Chidestudypress@gmail.com
Website: chidestudypress.com.au

Cover design:
Banjo Paterson - $10 banknote
Dundas Crawford, O'Brien, *What Ho, Crawford*, p.194.
Ah Wong, P.J.Travers, Frontspiece
Trip to Chinatown, *Sunday Times* 16 August 1896, p.2.

… a wrongly but highly civilised people

Ovens and Murray Advertiser, 7 March 1863, p.2.

Contents

Introduction

For much of our evidence on Chinese Australian history – especially in the 19th century – reliance is necessarily on European observers and European records. A great deal of this material is patronising at best and stereotypical or even plain made up at worst. In general, such observation pieces often tell us more about the writers than those being observed – although this too can be useful. Nevertheless, amid this diverse material can be found many instances of careful and interesting observation – even when it is patronising (and/or ignorant). Personal observation when sincerely given can provide much of value.

Presented here is a small selection of the abundant amount of such material to be found scattered throughout 19th century Australian sources. The selections range from the comments of a naive English teacher to those of an experienced China consul. From eyewitness to the arrival of the first 150 Chinese gold seekers to pass through Bathurst in 1855, as well as the astonished spectator to a Chinese opera. Not to mention the creations of the authors of both *Mary Poppins* and *The Man from Snowy River*. Of course, these sections would not be complete with reports from one each of those instant experts – the journalist and the travel writer.

No 1: *My Chinese* by Margaret Egerton

This fictionalised account of a European Australian woman's interactions with a group of Chinese Australians in the late 19th

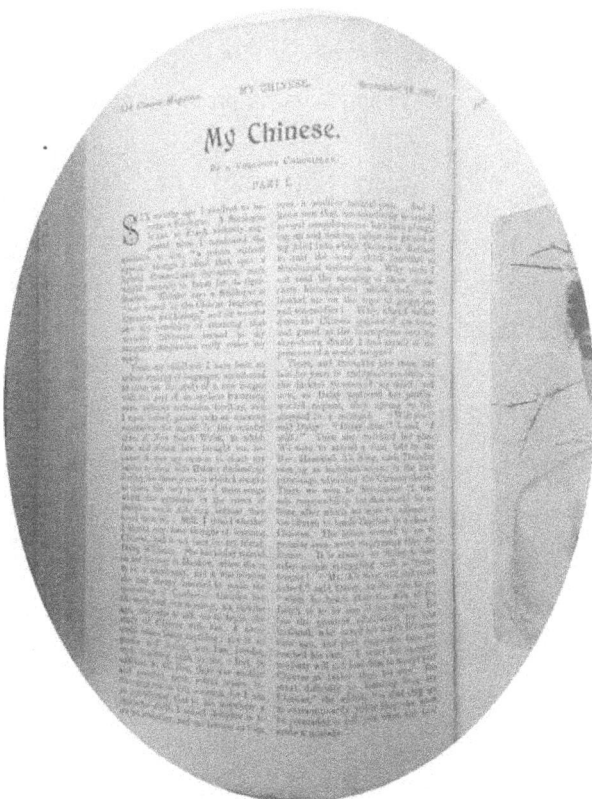

century was one my first discoveries as I began researching Chinese Australian history in the late 20th century.[1] The strong likelihood of its autobiographical nature was later confirmed by

---

[1] This would have been for Sojourn in Your Native Land, M.Litt, 1998. Now published in a revised edition in 2024.

another long-term researcher in the field Kate Bagnall when she recognised that the names of the children of the fictional "Rev Ah Sing" were in fact the same as the children of the real life Rev Young Wai.[2]

Margaret Egerton was thus one of those long and continuing line of Christian helpers in churches who provide English lessons to new arrivals in Australia in the hope that they will also convert to Christianity. [3] The article is however thankfully not much concerned with religion but rather with her observations of her English students and general remarks on Chinese people in late 19th century Australia.

The writer is fully aware of the embedded sense of class, superiority of civilisation, and no doubt 'race' of her readers. The result is a subtle poking of fun at these pretensions, though by no means a rejection of the stereotyping of Chinese people in Australia upon which much of the essay rests. Nevertheless, *My Chinese* is worth reading for its many astute observations and mild ironies, even if the ending is perhaps a little too cliched.

Having first read *My Chinese* some 25 years ago I am aware of how much my perceptions have broadened since. As a young

---

[2] K. Bagnall, *Golden shadows on a white land*, p.84.
[3] For a more robust form of Christian dealings with 'pagans' see *Chinese Australian History in 88 Objects*: No 2: Torn poster of a Chinese God

researcher I was looking for fodder for my work and mostly saw this article in terms of its hints of relationships, levels of English and other such specifics. Re-reading it now, I am much more aware of the subtle digs the writer is making at her own class and 'race', albeit while utilising a stereotypical view of her Chinese characters to do so. Margaret Egerton was writing for the amusement not education of her white audience after all.

The article tells us therefore – as many of these European observer articles do – more about the writer's prejudices and attitudes than it does about the Chinese people being discussed. These European prejudices and attitudes are a significant element of Chinese Australian history, and one such significant element with which the article begins is the 'missionary'. It is the narrator's friend who wishes to learn Chinese so she can travel to China and convert people to her brand of Christianity.[4] And it is from a convert to Christianity, now a minister in a Christian church, that they strive learn Chinese in exchange for teaching English to a class of Chinese market gardeners.

Before the lady can proceed to her class however, it is her husband who first presents us with some of the commonplace prejudices of his class and race. He begins by giving his views on Chinese people and culture, including that it is 'impossible of

---

[4] For more on the Rev Young Wai see Chinese Christian Churches (https://www.heritagecorridor.org.au) and 88 Objects: No.82 for some Australian missionary connections with China.

7

accomplishment' for anyone to learn 40,000 characters. But his most fundamental objection is that they are 'a dirty race', and the would-be student/teacher is only allowed to proceed on a promise of taking all proper 'sanitary precautions'. These precautions seem to be mostly of a perfumery nature and it is the subversion of these precautions that provides the story's climax.

While her husband demonstrates the cruder prejudices, it is the narrator's more subtle ones that are also challenged. Amazingly the first of these is the idea that Chinese people are 'unemotional'. This is a prejudice that apparently began with missionaries in China who it seems found the locals insufficiently moved by what they had to say and put this down to a lack of emotional capacity. While this prejudice is easily disposed of by the obvious family emotions on display as they enter the Minister's home, another regarding music is left in place or even re-enforced. Though that unmusicality could also lie on the other side is intimated.[5]

As an aside, we are given a dig at mansplaining to remind us that some things never change, before the origins of the writer's sympathy for Chinese people in Australia are hinted at. The first is her vague objection to the poll tax – or perhaps it is that working class people are the ones demanding this – that leads to an exchange of presents with her regular vegetable hawker. The

[5] Attitudes to music were largely determined by Chinese Opera, common in Australia at the time. See *Smoking opium, puffing cigars, and drinking gingerbeer: Chinese Opera in Australia* where emotion is also discussed.

second is witnessing her father's defence of a Chinese person from a group of larrikins.[6] Here the writer appears at her most naively unselfconscious as the account reeks of paternalism.

It is in Margaret Egerton's descriptions of her English students that we learn more as the individuals are introduced. The moonstruck Cum Lee and the student of medicine Paul Fee Lee, among others. All remain well within the stereotype of the humble, friendly market gardener and vegetable hawkers that most European Australians would have been familiar with – no hint of the real Rev Young Wai students some of whom became multinational businessmen.[7]

Of note is that while the difference between Cantonese and Mandarin languages is clear, the discovery of the tones necessary for adequate understanding in speaking comes rather late in her lessons.

The somewhat cliched climax of *My Chinese* is the miraculous cure of the narrator's neuralgia by a medical concoction she is too polite to refuse, despite her horror at the unhygienic way it is prepared.

---

[6] Larrikins at this time being gangs of youths happy to beat people up and destroy property rather than the lovable rouges of modern imagining. One of the English students is often pelted with stones by larrikins.

[7] See 88 Objects: No.79: Big Four and more in Shanghai. Also No.36 & No.39.

Overall, *My Chinese* is a reminder of the limits of mere politeness and toleration. The Chinese subjects of the story remain foils to allow the author to make subtle digs at her own class and Egerton is as disinclined (incapable?) of seeing past her own paternalism and prejudice as her readers. Not a stone throwing larrikin but a woman of her times just the same.

Despite these limitations, careful reading of such material as that offered by the somewhat naïve Mrs Egerton can be of value, even if only in informing us better of the mainstream community on which much of our evidence for Chinese Australian history, at least in the 19th century, is forced to rely.

Source
Margaret Egerton, "My Chinese", *The Cosmos Magazine*, Part I, 19 September 1896, pp.124-128, Part II, 19 October, pp.138-141, Part III, 19 November 1896, pp.192-196.[8]

---

[8] *The Cosmos Magazine* only ran from 1894 to 1899, though it did survive the arrest for fraud in 1896 of its originator, Armand Jerome. A hard copy is in the NSW State Library and a pdf version on the 88 Objects website. (Apologies for the poor image quality – the issues are bound in volumes and the pages will not lie flat. If anyone cares to do a transcript, I am happy to host it.)

No.2: The Man from Shanghae,
J Dundas Crawford

As the various Australian colonies developed their anti-Chinese
immigration attitudes and then laws, their British imperial
overseers took a keen interest. In general, the imperial attitude

James Dundas Crawford , ca 1877.
(Crawford Naughton Collection)

From: Bob O'Brien, *What Ho, Crawford, Old Chap: an
Anglo-Scot Interpreter (1850-1903)*, Dorset Enterprises,
Wellington, 2004.

was that such restrictions were a bad idea. Cheap labour was best, and why offend governments such as the Chinese or Japanese?

As part of this oversight the British Foreign Office sent out one of its people – James Dundas Crawford – who had some knowledge of the Chinese and even spoke Mandarin. Dundas Crawford was sent at a time when the Colony of Queensland was concerned by thousands of Chinese goldseekers arriving at Cooktown and walking inland to the Palmer River goldfields. This was in 1877 and the report of his observations of Chinese activity in Queensland, NSW and Victoria was duly sent to the British Foreign Office.

The report makes fascinating reading. It is not only a rare example of a wide-ranging investigation with many interesting comments but even rarer, it is written in a, for the times, objective and sensible manner. Despite this, the Crawford report remains an underutilised resource. Historians have done what they all too often do with interesting material, plunder it for a quote or statistic relevant to their specific task and then leave the remains to languish in a footnote. It was in a footnote I found the Crawford report many years ago and intrigued I tracked down a the copy of the voluminous British Foreign Office files kept in the National Library of Australia.

After reading it I did two things that I am repeating here. The first is to make the full report – it is only 33 pages long – available for people to read in its full Victorian glory (long sentences and patronising tone mostly). Secondly, I wrote an article that basically described the Crawford report and provided some context in the hope of encouraging its wider use as a source. While its wider use has certainly occurred, this aspect could perhaps be improved still.

A rather whimsical representation of the trek to the Palmer River goldfields.
Australasian Sketcher, 12 June 1875, p.8.

Why do I like the Crawford report so much? Mainly because in a period when there is virtually no Chinese voice to be found, Crawford's outsider view (outside the white colonial concerns of the colonies) provides us with the next best thing. At one point Crawford even spoke before a crowd of European miners in Victoria on behalf of Chinese miners 'urging their claims to be allowed to mine on the rush'.[9]

---

[9] *Bendigo Advertiser*, 24 March 1877, p.3.

13

Nevertheless, Crawford was by no means a modern multiculturalist, but he does give us an analysis that is closer to the Chinese perspective than nearly anything else we get until the beginning of the Chinese language press in Australia some twenty years later. Furthermore, I think people should read sources directly rather than be reliant on the interpretation of academics – something modern technology now makes so much easier.

Enjoy!

The full text of the report can be found on the 88 Objects website:

The Crawford Report, Shanghae 1877
Great Britain, Foreign Office Confidential Prints: No.3742, *Notes by Mr. Crawford on Chinese Immigration in the Australian Colonies*, J. Dundas Crawford, 1 September 1877.

[https://chinozhistory.org/wp-content/uploads/2021/06/Crawford-report.pdf]

For my write up on the Crawford Report:

Michael Williams, 'Observations of a China Consul', *Locality*, Vol. 11, no.2, 2000, pp. 24-31.

[https://webarchive.nla.gov.au/awa/20050713004607/http://pandora.nla.gov.au/pan/20743/20050712-0000/131.172.16.7/pdf/crawford.pdf]

Corrections – a few years after I wrote my piece on the Crawford report a publication utilising many of Dundas Crawford's letters to his family allows some clarifications. This was: Bob O'Brien, *What Ho, Crawford, Old Chap: an Anglo-Scot Interpreter (1850-1903)*, Dorset Enterprises, Wellington, 2004.

- I discussed why the British sent Crawford. However, in a letter home he claims it was his idea. Certainly, he was disappointed the report did not lead to anything.
- I speculated about whether or not Crawford spoke Cantonese but in a letter to his sister he makes clear he spoke only Mandarin but that he was able to use this in Australia nevertheless as well as English.

Who was James Dundas Crawford?

His seems in many ways a sad story. His mother died when he was two, then he was shipped off to distant relatives before Eton at 7 years of age. His father went to New Zealand as a magistrate while he joined the British Consular Service. Not long after returning to Shanghai and submitting his report Dundas Crawford suffered a mental breakdown and spent the rest of his life living quietly in England before dying aged 52 in 1903.

For more on the Palmer River Goldrush see:

Noreen Kirkman, *Chinese Miners on the Palmer* (Presented to a meeting of the Society 28 August 1986).

No.3: Amazing the yokels of Bathurst

Much of the history of Chinese Australia seems about hostility

and racism, or attempts to subvert and overcome these negatives. But at one point in the history Chinese people were simply exotic arrivals from a foreign land. Before the (white) locals could begin adopting stereotypes or making up reasons to reject those who were different they were confronted with people who were merely different.[10] For example, there are hints of sheer honest amazement at Chinese culture and civilization piecing through the narrow assumptions of British/Christian superiority in some of the accounts of Chinese Opera in 19th century Australia.[11] But outside these

[10] What stereotype is this? Illustration by Frederick Grosse, section from 'Arrival of Chinese immigrants in Little Bourke Street', *The Australian News for Home Readers*, 27 September 1866.

[11] For example, Local Intelligence – Chinese Opera, *Ovens and Murray Advertiser*, 7 March 1863, p.2, where the critic is both 'astonished and pleased'. For more on Chinese Opera in Australia see "Smoking opium, puffing cigars, and drinking gingerbeer: Chinese Opera in Australia".

scattered examples a pervasive smug condescension holds sway. However, early in the NSW goldrushes the small, relatively isolated settlement of Bathurst, only a generation after it war with the surrounding Aboriginal peoples[12], found itself presented with some 150 Chinese men walking to the nearby goldfields. This well organised company were the cause of much excited for the locals and crowds of them came to the camping area to gawk at the newcomers. An account of this spectacle gives us some idea of how things were when two groups of strangers met for the first time without yet any history of antagonism or the need to throw up self-justifying prejudices.

> Our diggings promise to become the sites of a series of Chinese colonies. A few days ago a second batch of the sons of the Celestial Empire arrived in Bathurst, consisting, as nearly as we can guess, of about 150, and proceeded to the camping ground of their predecessors, where they pitched their tents, spread their mats, and commenced cooking — , favourite pastime apparently, which, together with eating, seems to swallow up the whole day. Amongst their number we perceived several rather ancient looking pig-tails, who, in all probability, have come to deposit their bones in Australia. Their canvass village has been a favourite resort for the townspeople, who have thronged in front of their tents to witness the novelty of their proceedings, amongst which the expert use of their chopsticks was not the least amusing. Their economical use of firewood was another circumstance which called forth the astonishment of the visitors, who saw that by digging small holes in the ground, with ventilation only in front, that about as much timber was consumed in boiling and

---

[12] See, Stephen Gapps, *Gudyarra: The First Wiradyuri War of Resistance — The Bathurst War, 1822–1824.*

stewing for 150 as would cook a meal for a single family, after our own fashion. There was the usual display of fans and purses, and other trifles for sale, but the exorbitant prices asked reduced their traffic almost to nil. On Monday last they struck their tents, and trotted off to the westward with their stock of domestic utensils, mats, and bedding, slung upon poles.[13]

There is little here of the fear and loathing or the heavy patronising tone that would become commonplace. On the other hand, there is also no hint that practices which, for example, would reduce the consumption of firewood to an extraordinary degree might be worth imitating. The arrival of this group is an interesting spectacle but it is not one that could impinge upon the habits and prejudices brought ready made from Europe. The scene is set for that 'othering' that would make up so much of subsequent Chinese Australian history.

The Bathurst Free Press
AND MINING JOURNAL.

For more on Chinese Australian history on the NSW Goldfields see:

88 Objects, Pieces of 8: Bathurst 8
[https://chinozhistory.org/index.php/bathurst-8/]

See, Juanita Kwok and Ely Finch, *Bew Chip's Register: A Chinese Australian Remittance Register*, Tambaroora and Hill End Goldfield.

---

[13] *Bathurst Free Press and Mining Journal*, 30 July 1856, p.2. Thanks to Juanita Kwok for spotting this gem quoted in her excellent thesis, Juanita Kwok, *The Chinese in Bathurst: Recovering Forgotten Histories*, Doctoral thesis, Charles Sturt University, Bathurst, 2018.

Mew Chip who lived most of his life at Hill End would have passed through Bathurst.

Holtermann Collection,
State Library of NSW

No.4: A night at the Opera

Chinese Opera is one of those cultural forms that are both deeply embedded in its culture and generally perceived by outsiders as a most exotic and relatively inaccessible representation of that culture. Yet for well over 50 years

Illustrated Australian News for Home Readers (Melbourne), 16 July 1872, p.144.

'Chinese Opera' (Pear Garden or Great Drama in Chinese) was performed regularly in Australia to such an extent that English language scripts were handed out and Chinese Opera related sayings were part of Australian slang.[14]

---

[14] For example, dogs at the 1928 Longreach Show were described as creating a "din, that a Chinese opera company would give half its life to accomplish". *The Longreach Leader*, 2 March 1928, p.21.

Subsequent 'whitewashing' of Australian history has erased the community memory of this entertainment as it has much else related to non-white Australian history. Despite the long history of Chinese Opera in Australia there is very little evidence from Chinese people themselves and we are forced to rely on European accounts of these performances. [15] As with other European observations of Chinese activity in Australia these accounts are a mix of ignorance, earnest desc ription, stereotyping, fascination and patronising tones. However, the nature of Chinese Opera, representing as it does a 'high' cultural form had the capacity to

Extract from: "At a Chinese Opera," *Queenslander* (Brisbane), 11 June 1904, p.41. By artist Hal Eyre.

---

[15] Some of the few are, *Tung Wah News*, 19 October 1898, p.4, *The Chinese Australian Herald*, 9 November 1894, p.5, and *The Chinese Australian Herald*, 6 February 1904, p.5.

cut through some of the sense of cultural superiority that nearly always characterised 19th century European commentators. Thus, we have in these descriptions of Chinese Opera performance in Australia the closest these British/European/Christian/white (male) [16] observers could come to admitting an 'other' culture might have something to offer or at least to acknowledging a near equality. Even if often somewhat backhanded:

> The decorations and dresses displayed a high degree of barbaric taste, for although we could recognise the uncouth ideas of a wrongly but highly civilised people, there was nothing that would strike the most fastidious taste as being senseless or vulgar.[17]

In 1872 a Melbourne observer contrasted the insight opera gave into the upper echelons of Chinese culture unfavorably with their impression of the local Chinatown:

> A visit to the theatre in the Chinese quarter is exceedingly interesting as the performance altogether gives a higher idea of the manners and customs of the flowery land than a cursory glance at Little Bourke street.[18]

In Brisbane in 1894, it was the stage that amazed and the:

> greatest [set] change was the raising of a mountain which a fleeing warrior and his wife had to cross. This was done by three tables and half-a-dozen chairs piled on each other and surmounted by an artificial bough fixed to the back of a chair.[19]

---

[16] Self-identification varied then as now.

[17] "Local Intelligence – Chinese Opera," *Ovens and Murray Advertiser*, 7 March 1863, p.2.

[18] *Illustrated Australian News for Home Readers*, 16 July 1872, p.144.

[19] *The Telegraph*, 3 September 1894, p.5; *The Brisbane Courier*, 3 September 1894, 5.

A Chinese language newspaper published in Sydney reported in 1898 that Europeans spectators where common and on at least one occasion appeared in the cast.[20] Moreover, a performance of "eight Western beauties" "dancing like swallows" appeared that same year.[21] While a generation before in the Victorian goldfields town of Ararat, Europeans had joined the performers:

> With faces fiercely painted, and robed in the floweriest of dresses, they strutted and ruffled their fans and wooden swords in a manner that brought down the house enthusiastically.[22]

This is just a small taste of the many observations of Chinese Opera as it was performed from Tasmania to Cairns and many places in between throughout 19th century and into early 20th century Australia. What is remarkable it not that it happened but that it has largely been forgotten that it happened.

For a detailed account of Chinese Opera in Australia see:

Michael Williams, "Smoking opium, puffing cigars, and drinking gingerbeer: Chinese Opera in Australia", in *Opera, Emotion, and the Antipodes Volume II Applied Perspectives: Compositions and Performances*, edited by Jane W. Davidson, Michael Halliwell and Stephanie Rocke, pp.166-208. Abingdon: Routledge, 2020.

---

[20] *Tung Wah News*, 19 October 1898, p.4.

[21] *Tung Wah News*, 19 October 1898, p.4.

[22] *Mount Alexander Mail*, 16 November 1864, p.3.

CHINESE OPERA.

HOW IT IS WRITTEN AND STAGED.

(BY F. J. C.)

譜	笛

笛 (風入松):

上上工上 工上 五丁
上上工尺 工尺 五丁工尺
五上尺工 尺工 上尺工
五上 五上尺 上尺五
丁五上丁 尺丁五上
工尺丁工 尺工五上丁
尺丁工尺 丁工五上
上 工尺 尺五工

譜:

上上工何士上何
上士何工 士何上
工何士工何 取魚
士何工何 尺上上工尺
何士上 尺上工尺尺
尺工尺 尺工上
何士 何士上
上 上士何

Evening News, 29 April 1904, p.7.

25

No.5: Ah Wong meets Mary Poppins

Unsurprisingly Chinese Australian characters pop up from time to time in 20th century Australian literature and just as unsurprisingly these are usually stock characters – a cook, a miner, a gambler or

a gardener, but rarely a father, husband or son and even less likely a mother or daughter. [23] As a result little is revealed about the motivations or intentions of such characters. This is natural in works by authors who would have understood little, like most of their contemporary European Australians, about the motivations or

Ah Wong

---

[23] Cheon the cook in *We of the Never Never* or Ah Soon the vegetable hawker in Henry Lawson's *Ah Soon: A Chinese-Australian Story* for example. The great exception to this in Australian literature are the mothers, wives and husbands that appear in *The Poison of Polygamy* written by (not European) Wong Shee Ping.

intentions of their fellow Chinese Australians. People that most would not have felt, until deep into the 20th century at least, were in fact their fellow Australians.

Nevertheless, writers often write from personal experience and something can be gleaned from their observations even when sieved through prejudice and ignorance. One such example it may surprise to learn is by P. L. Travers (the Australian-born author of the Mary Poppins stories) who wrote an interesting and

P. L. Travers

for her times sympathetic account of her childhood association with a Chinese cook. Entitled simply *Ah Wong*, the story is not well known as Travers apparently produced it in a limited edition as a Christmas special in 1943 with the note:

This edition of Ah Wong is limited to five hundred copies privately printed for the friends of the author as a Christmas greeting.
A copy can be found in the NSW State Library however.[24]

The main character is Ah Wong, who takes care of the children of the family in rural Queensland that employs him, rejects their efforts to convert him to Christianity, and saves all his money. Travers grew up in rural Queensland and in all likelihood her family employed such a cook or certainly she knew families who

---

[24] P. L. Travers, *Ah Wong*, New York, High Grade Press, 1943.

did. Travers, child or adult, was ignorant as to why Ah Wong might save his money so earnestly, merely believing that he was saving to return to China:

All their lives they have saved their money so that they may have enough to take them home.

A very low income and a very high passenger fare it would seem. In reality of course men such as Ah Wong were supporting their own families in China, and if they grew old and/or were impoverished, they might receive assistance from district-based societies to pay their fare home. Unlike the ship Ah Wong takes that is seemingly full only of aged men, many men when younger also visited their family in China. Returning to Australia after a few years with their Certificate Exempting From Dictation Test (CEDT's) to work again for a number of years.[25]

After the death of her father Travers moved to Sydney and wrote for various journals and newspapers. The second half of the Ah Wong story has the girl from Queensland working as a journalist in Sydney where by chance she meets her childhood cook Ah Wong. Once again neither Travers or her journalist character has much idea of the motivations or life story of men like Ah Wong. What was known was the Chinese men traveling through the Port of Sydney by ship to and from China was common. That many by the early 20th century were old and that some returned to China

---

[25] For a detailed account of this lifestyle see, Michael Williams, *Returning home with glory: Chinese villagers around the Pacific, 1849 to 1949*, Hong Kong University Press, Hong Kong, 2018.

for a final trip after a lifetime working in Australia would also have been general knowledge at the time. And this is what we are told Ah Wong is doing - taking ship in Sydney to finally return to China.

Only republished in 2014, *Ah Wong* is a fascinating addition to our Chinese Australian literature. However, while it can be categorised as "sympathetic" despite its stereotyping, this only highlights the limitations of sympathy without knowledge. For Travers, Ah Wong can only be written as an amusing two-dimensional character with none of the insights her Mary Poppin's characters display. As yet the closest to such insights apart from *The Poison of Polygamy* already mentioned is not a work of literature but of oral history – the recently published *South Flows the Pearl* is a fine addition to much need individual insight into Chinese Australian history.

Further reading

Wong Shee Ping, (Ely Finch, trans),
The Poison of Polygamy - A Social Novel, University of Sydney Press, 2019.

Mavis Yen, (Siaoman Yen & Richard Horsburgh, eds), *South Flows the Pearl*, (Sydney University Press, 2022).

No. 6: A white women in Chinatown

One of the most widespread leitmotifs in Chinese Australian history is the perception of Chinese people as a mysterious group whose

A

TRIP TO CHINATOWN

THAT DID COME OFF.

The Dens Described by a Lady Journalist.

communities and activities needed to be 'interpreted' by special investigations or self-appointed experts. Thus, an article in the *Sunday Times* 16 August 1896, p.2, entitled "A TRIP TO CHINATOWN" is merely one of a long series of similar efforts by sensation seeking newspapers. Only its subtitle, *The Dens Described by a Lady Journalist* hints that this one might be different. However, this proves a false hope and not only is the article typical of its kind but its relentless sexism encourages the possibility that it was in fact written, or at least heavily edited, by a male pretending to be a female.

Regardless of the gender of the journalist this account of a visit to Chinatown is typical of the observations and judgements made about Chinese people living in Australia around the turn of the 20th century. *Dens Described by a Lady Journalist* runs through nearly every cliché in the European Australian guidebook of Chinese Australians. Thus, we get a 'Chinatown' right from the get go, murder, gambling, the need for a police escort, dismissive remarks about religion, opium smoking of course, vegetable hawkers and cleanliness, politeness, exotic cooking, mixed race, and to justify the 'lady journalist' angle, that great dread, the supposed Chinese desire for, and corruption of, white women.

'Chinatown' has ghetto connotations that simply describing a poorer area of Sydney with a concentration of Chinese people and businesses, but nevertheless inhabited by many non-Chinese people does not. The 'Chinatown' concept at this time having been imported from San Francisco and bringing a ready-made sense of the exotic.

On arrival under police escort in this 'exotic' Sydney location – the streets near the then Belmore Markets (now the Capitol Theatre) – a murder is immediately alluded to. Though this crime appears to be merely for the purposes of adding atmosphere as it is unrelated to anything that follows. Next a gambling shop is briefly visited to add more colour to the investigation, though no mention is made of the fact that such places had a high proportion of European customers. After this a 'Joss' is described – that is a temple or at least a shrine to a Chinese god – in the kinds of dismissive terms that came effortlessly to late 19th century Christians.

This is all preliminary to the arrival at an opium den, which while very much legal at this time would soon cease to be so. Legal or illegal such 'dens' held much fascination for newspaper readers and like gambling were often frequented by non-Chinese. In fact, two such non-Chinese customers are cited, including one who is allowed to make a prophesy that 'an advance of civilisation' would see opium 'classified with tobacco smoking'.

IMPLEMENTS FOR OPIUM SMOKING.
1 Opium box——2 Wet rag for cooling opium pipe——3 Opium pipe——4 Chinese tobacco pipe. 5 Lamp-glass made from ordinary bottle——6 Lamp——7 Scissors for trimming lamp.

Gambling and opium cover the two main vices attributed to all Chinese people at the time. These vices could be easily denounced as 'wrong' by those inclined to make such judgments while reading a newspaper.

More difficult to evaluate was the success of Chinese people at selling vegetables to those same readers, their well-known politeness when doing so, the deliciousness of their food, and the tendency of white women to marry them and produce children of mixed heritage. All these are dealt with in a manner typical of the period, including damming with faint praise and the introduction of carping asides.

Thus, the recognisably 'fine cabbages and cauliflowers' are kept in conditions that makes the writer 'thankful for the efficacy of boiling water'. The politeness is perhaps due to simplicity. While the cooking is undoubtedly 'nice' and 'dainty' looking but only leads to 'hastily swallowing a eucalyptus lozenge'. Finally, to 'a rather striking-looking woman, a half-caste Chinese with a suggestion of Semitic origin' is attributed what cleanliness is apparent.

It is the appearance of this woman of Chinese/European heritage that sets off a puzzled denunciation of mixed relationships. It is well known apparently that 'they [Chinese men] prefer Europeans speaking generally' while that they are 'most kind and considerate' is dismissed rather weirdly 'as but the outcome of the Asiatic philosophy'. It follows from such a flawless argument that any association with 'white women' must be 'prolific of the utmost degradation'. The prejudiced ranting and confusion of emotion with logic carries on for a while more but to no better effect until the journalistic investigation reaches its denouement when a real live white women, or girl in this case, is found in the clutches of the Chinese.

The readers are obviously not ready for any realistic account of the vulnerability of young women in their society and instead are presented with a foolish girl whose loving family will take her back in a heartbeat. All that is necessary is a few words from a gruff but kindly policeman and a 'women who understand women' and her escape is assured. Any support or assistance shown by the Chinese man is mere entrapment and so the basic goodness and sanity of white society is maintained.

The readers of such articles were presumably titillated and shocked enough to feel safe in their world while not actually learning anything to disturb their prejudices. If there is anything wrong in the world it must be the fault of the Chinese. Such writing was common and served to reenforce the stereotypes and justifications for the then evolving White Australia policy. It would be nice to feel that such pitiable journalism was the preserve of the late 19th century only but anyone who still reads newspapers, let alone more modern forms of media, knows this is sadly not the case.

OPIUM SMOKERS' BUNKS.
8 Combined chair, lounge, and bed——9 Pillow.

No. 7: To the goldfields by Omnibus

Among the many stereotypes of people of Chinese origin in Australia that existed a common one was that they were extremely frugal and could and did live off earnings that anyone else (usually meaning white men) would starve on.

A ST. KILDA OMNIBUS ON SUNDAY.
Conductor.—"JUMP UP SIR—LOTS O' ROOM."

This stereotype fitted well with the idea that Chinese workers were "unfair" competition and hence it was justified that they be discriminated against in various ways. As is usual, once equipped with a stereotype observers and writers for newspapers would complacently spot and repeat circumstances that confirmed the stereotype. Much rarer was the objective observer who reported what they actually saw even when it contradicted the received wisdom.

One such case was William Kelly who made his living from travelling the world and writing books describing the exotic locations he had been to. And in the middle of the 19th century there were few such places more exotic as far as his English based readership was concerned than the goldfields of the new colony of Victoria. Kelly made a number of interesting observations concerning the numerous Chinese people who had joined so many others from around the world to seek their fortunes by seeking for gold, but one of the most interesting was his observations as to the use of omnibuses:

> I have already shown that they do not practise self-denial at their board, and as a proof that they are equally liberal in their personal expenses, I have only to state that it is remarked that the omnibuses and public conveyances which ply about Sandhurst and in the Bendigo district are largely patronised by Chinese; in fact, it would be safe to wager, as one of these vehicles is approaching that one-third of the passengers are of Celestial origin. The same average, I am satisfied, would be tolerably correct with regard to the coaches running to Melbourne. I know I have been several times up and down the line, and on every occasion I had from three to six Chinese fellow passengers. On one of the journeys, occupying the box seat, the driver called my attention to the circumstance "that while we frequently passed parties of European diggers on their way to the town, toiling along under heavy swags, we never saw one solitary instance of Chinamen returning on foot" and such, he informed me, is invariably the case.[26]

Just why Chinese people were more inclined to take public transport than others it is impossible to say at this remove. Here it is important to note that not all sources are equal and much that we read in newspapers and books past is no more reliable than

---

[26] *Life in Victoria* by William Kelly, Esq. Note: Sandhurst = Ballarat

what appears in the media today. Reliance must be had on one's own judgement and it needs to be left to the reader to judge if William Kelly is more or less reliable.

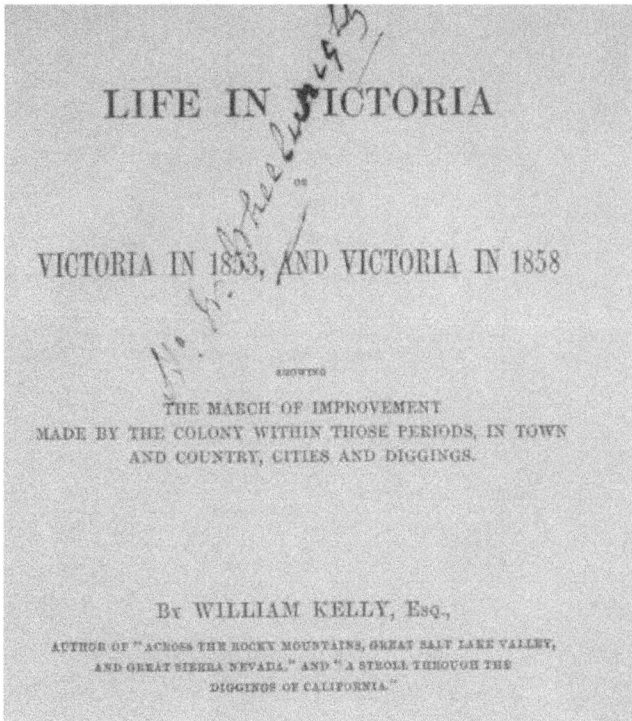

LIFE IN VICTORIA

OR

VICTORIA IN 1853, AND VICTORIA IN 1858

SHOWING

THE MARCH OF IMPROVEMENT
MADE BY THE COLONY WITHIN THOSE PERIODS, IN TOWN
AND COUNTRY, CITIES AND DIGGINGS.

By WILLIAM KELLY, Esq.,

AUTHOR OF "ACROSS THE ROCKY MOUNTAINS, GREAT SALT LAKE VALLEY,
AND GREAT SIERRA NEVADA," AND "A STROLL THROUGH THE
DIGGINGS OF CALIFORNIA."

No. 8: Jimmy the Pat

Characters of Chinese heritage appear in many works of
Australian literature, all too often as cooks or gardeners with little
personality and less background. They serve, like Ah Wong (see
No.6 above), as stereotypes rather than character studies.

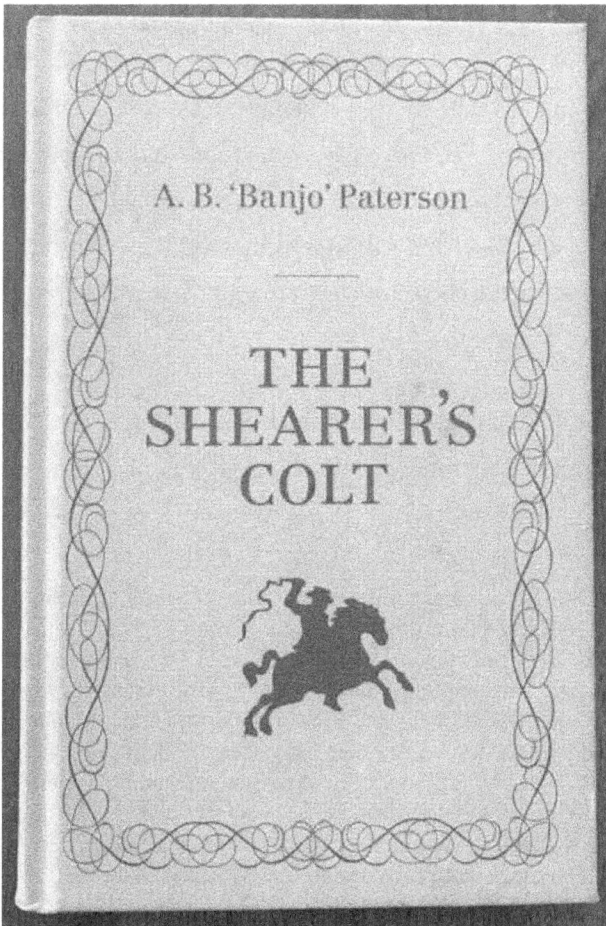

A. B. 'Banjo' Paterson

THE
SHEARER'S
COLT

Why this is the case ranges from the power of stereotypes to inhibit real knowledge, to the whitewashing of Australian history that took place throughout the 20th century. The result was not only the deletion of much of the role of Chinese Australians from Australian history but even making it to a large degree unimaginable.

In *The Shearer's Colt* written by Banjo Paterson in 1936 but set perhaps in the 1890s we have a similar stock Chinese character called Jimmy the Pat. Banjo Paterson is most well-known for his poetry but he also wrote a couple of novels and in this one Paterson introduces his character with such a focused blast of stereotypes and generalisations that it deserves mention as a classic of the genre.

This list of Jimmy's career highlights also tells us what a white Australian of Paterson's generation knew or thought they knew about Chinese Australians:

> "Don't you make any mistake," he said, "this is a wonderful chap, this Chow. He started with nothing—just a coolie—but he was a big, powerful bloke and could mix it with anybody. He was in the ring for a bit, what d'you think of that—a Chow in the ring! He could take a punch too, let me tell you. 'My face all same iun,' he'd say. Then he took on running fan-tan and pakapoo joints, and he got to be a big man, because if any of the larrikin crowd got playing up Jimmy could knock him cold. Then he started smuggling opium and working it back to the blacks and Chows up in the Territory—heaven only knows what he made out of that. Then he started importing Chinese coolies from Canton with false

identification papers, and he made these coolies work as slaves for him in Chinese gardens, until they had paid him big money. He owns a couple of stations on the quiet. And then, dash me, if he doesn't start bookmaking!"

"I'll tell you something," he said, "Jimmy's a very solid man and gives thousands to charities. But there's hardly a fan-tan shop or an opium joint in Queensland but what Jimmy's got a finger in it. There isn't a criminal in Queensland but what would do exactly what Jimmy told him and do it at the double. I think that he took up the bookmaking so that he could travel about and keep an eye on all sorts of crooked jobs. Anything from fan-tan to murder. I don't put anything past Jimmy. His right name is Kum Yoon Jim, but the boys call him Jimmy the Pat. They call all Chinamen 'Pat.' The larrikin crowd only call him that behind his back. He'll hit any one that calls him Pat to his face. Tough on the Irish, isn't it, when a Chinaman, will strike a man for calling him 'Pat'! It ought to be a compliment."

What Banjo Paterson has done here is compress into a single paragraph and a single person a great many of the elements of Chinese Australian history as perceived by European Australians. Thus we have the 'coolie' or labourer, gambling, opium, market gardening, and false papers. The idea of a Chinese boxer may well have come from the real life Rud Kee who worked with Jimmy Sharman for over 50 years. 'Pat' as a slang term for a Chinese person was common in the early 20th century, especially in sporting circles.[27] While finally, Paterson's grandfather Robert Barton likely had some indentured workers from Amoy on his Bathurst property in the 1850s.[28]

---

[27] See, *Sydney Sportsman*, 18 February 1920, p.1, Pinching the Pats. A CHINAMAN'S LUCK.

[28] For the reference to both Rud Kee and Robert Paterson the author thanks Dr Juanita Kwok.

Banjo Paterson was not being especially racist when he created Jimmy the Pat but he was drawing on the half-knowledge and stereotypes of his generation that would have made his readers readily accept this character. Yet Jimmy the Pat while a 'bad guy' is also a strong character who dominates his world. Paterson does not hesitate to do this as his generation did not necessarily see Chinese Australians as the unrelenting victims that another two generations of whitewashing would try to make the norm.

For less stereotypical views try the previously cited:

Bew Chip's Register

South Flows the Pearl

The Poison of Polygamy

More in the Pieces of 8 series

CHINATOWN 8 (SYDNEY)

MITCHELL LIBRARY 8

ZHONGSHAN 8

TASMANIAN 8

BATHURST 8

ASHFIELD 8

CHINESE VOICES 8

Forthcoming

SHANGHAI 8

STATE ARCHIVES 8 (NSW)

ROBE WALK 8

MISSING 8

CEMETARY 8

WOMENS 8

MEMORIAL 8

NORTHERN TERRITORY 8

MUSEUM 8

NATIONAL ARCHIVE 8

STATUES 8

CHINATOWN 8 (MELBOURNE)

FAKES & MYTHS 8

TRANSLATIONS 8

CHINESE NEWSPAPER ARTICLES 8

APPRECIATIONS 8

About *Chinese Australian History in 88 Objects*

This simple yet effective website showcases 88 objects from the history of the Chinese in Australia. It ranges over 200 years of migration history, illuminating political, social and economic aspects of the Chinese presence in the colonies and then Commonwealth. The objects come from both private and public institutions, each one including some discussion of its use and meaning in the past but also its curation and resonance today. Including bureaucratic forms and cafe menus, temple bells and even entire houses, this website provides readers with immediate access to a still overlooked part of the nation's formation.

The website is attractively designed and extremely easy to use — a reminder of the importance of thinking through universal accessibility to communicate with as wide an audience as possible. Its focus on the everyday stimulates users to think about the deeper histories and futures of other objects, both in Chinese–Australian history and in the history of other migrant groups. This beautiful portal promises only to grow richer as it finds more topics for investigation.

NSW Premiers Digital History Prize judge 2022

You can find

Chinese Australian History in 88 Objects

at

https://chinozhistory.org

About the author

Michael Williams, Adjunct Professor at the Institute for Australian and Chinese Arts and Culture (IAC), Western Sydney University, is a scholar of Chinese-Australian history and a founding member of the Chinese-Australian Historical Society. He is the author of *Returning Home with Glory* (HKU Press, 2018), *Australia's Dictation Test: The test it was a Crime to Fail* (Brill, 2021) and *Every requisite for a campaign upon the gold-fields* (Chidestudy Press, 2024). His website: Chinese Australian History in 88 Objects was shortlisted for the 2022 Premiers Digital History Prize. Michael is currently Project Manager of the Scattered Legacy project, a national database of Chinese Australian history.

Basic introduction to Chinese-Australian history

While there is much written on Chinese people in Australia much of it is outdated or based on stereotypes. In the last 20 years or so a great deal of new research has added much of value to our understanding. However, there is still no one standard work that covers all of this history in any useful manner. Listed below is a selection of excellent works that together cover a broad range of this history. Anyone of these well researched pieces will help you cut through the stereotypes that continue to predominate this history.

On women
Kate Bagnall, 'Rewriting the history of Chinese families in nineteenth-century Australia', *Australian Historical Studies*, vol. 42, no. 1, March 2011: pp.62–77.

On radicalism
Gregor Benton, "Australia", pp.72-91 in *Chinese Migrants and Internationalism: Forgotten Histories, 1917–1945* (Rutledge, 2007).

On the environment
Sheng Fei, "Environmental Experiences of Chinese People in the Mid-Nineteenth Century Australian Gold Rushes," *Global Environment*, 2011, 7/8: 111.

On politics
John Fitzgerald, *Big White Lie,* Sydney: UNSW Press, 2007.

On the North
Natalie Fong, The Significance of the Northern Territory in the Formulation of 'White Australia' Policies, 1880–1901, *Australian Historical Studies*, 49:4, 2018, pp.527-545.

On business
Peter Gibson, "Australia's Bankrupt Chinese Furniture Manufacturers, 1880–1930", *Australian Economic History Review*, 2018, 58: pp.87-107.

On merchants
Mei-fen Kuo, *Making Chinese Australia: Urban Elites, Newspapers and the Formation of Chinese Australian Identity, 1892–1912* (Clayton, Victoria: Monash University Publishing 2013).

On North Queensland
Cathie May, *Topsawyers: The Chinese in Cairns 1870–1920*,
        (Townsville: James Cook University Press, 1984).

On miners
Barry McGowan, "The Economics and Organisation of Chinese Mining
        in Colonial Australia", *Australian Economic History Review*,
        2005, 45: pp.119-138.

On south China villages
Michael Williams, *Returning Home with Glory: Chinese Villagers
        around the Pacific, 1849 to 1949* (Hong Kong: Hong Kong
        University Press, 2018).

On coolie myths
Sophie Loy-Wilson, "Coolie alibis: Seizing gold from Chinese miners
        in New South Wales", *International Labor and Working Class
        History,* 2017, 91, pp.28-45.

On Chinese Australian literature
Wong Shee Ping, (Ely Finch, trans), *The Poison of Polygamy - A Social
        Novel*, University of Sydney Press, 2019.

On oral history
Mavis Yen, (Siaoman Yen & Richard Horsburgh, eds), *South Flows the
        Pearl,* (Sydney University Press, 2022).

On being a classic
C. F. Yong, *The New Gold Mountain: the Chinese in Australia, 1901-
        1921* (Richmond, S. Aust: Raphael Arts, 1977).

Also available at *ChideStudy Press*

Of the many episodes that make up the oftentimes exotic impression of Chinese Australian history the 1850s walk from the small port of Robe in South Australia to the goldfields of Victoria has repeatedly taken on epic proportions. Its 'long march' like length, tales of hardship and death, not to mention present-day outrage at the discriminatory tax the walk was designed to avoid, all combine to make the stuff of legends.

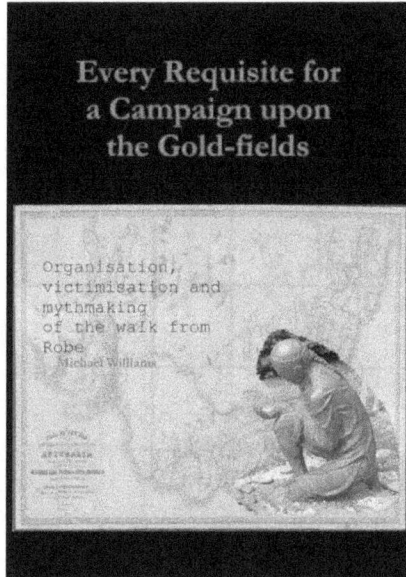

Every Requisite for a Campaign upon the Gold-fields

Organisation, victimisation and mythmaking of the walk from Robe
Michael Williams

Yet remarkably the telling of this history has largely been left to local historians with their characteristic eagerness to retell every tale and make use of every allusion to their subject with little regard to plausibility, contradiction or even relevance. Thus, while the arrival of thousands of gold seekers from southern China in the mid-1850s at Robetown on Guichen Bay, South Australia, in order to avoid taxes imposed by the neighbouring gold rich colony of Victoria is well known, it is surprisingly little understood in detail.

Brief Sojourn in Your Native Land highlights the enduring connection between Sydney and South China from the late 19th century to the mid-20th century, maintained by thousands of Sydney residents born in the diverse districts of the Pearl River Delta of southern China. The work draws on Immigration Restriction Act files, the Royal Commission on Alleged Chinese Gambling, the burial register of the Chinese section of Rookwood Cemetery, and oral histories from descendants of these residents. The narrative reveals the experiences of a generation often referred to as *huaqiao*, whose ties to their home villages are traced from youth through adulthood and into retirement, passing onto subsequent generations. Throughout their lives, the huaqiao were largely driven by a desire to support their families in their home villages, fostering ties between these villages and Sydney that lasted for at least two generations.

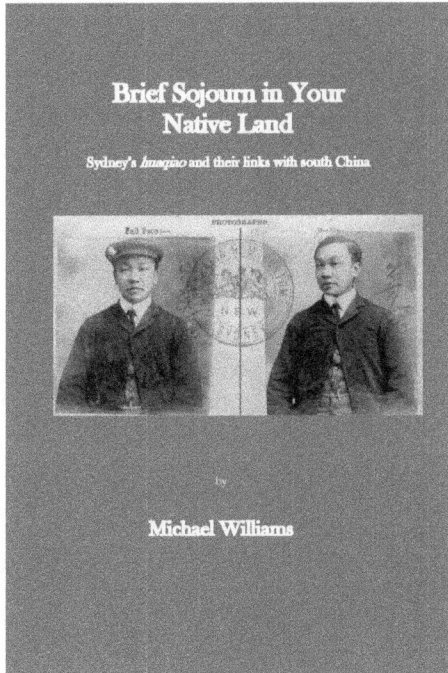

Chinese Voices 8 – Vol 2 in the **Pieces of 8** series

Having read what European Australian's had to say about Chinese Australians now is your chance to read what Chinese Australian had to say about themselves.

Ranging from the first (certainly the earliest extant) piece of Chinese writing in Australia as an indentured shepherd named Ang defends himself in 1850 from a murder charge, to a 1910 novel written in Literary Chinese on the eve of China's Republican revolution by the Melbourne based Wong Shee Ping. There are also reasoned attacks on discriminatory legislation, personal memoirs old and new, poetry, letters from relations back in the village, and short stories expressing something of life in "white" Australia for someone of non-white heritage.

Together these 'Chinese Voices 8' provide a fascinating insight into some of the many facets of Chinese Australian history as spoken to us by Chinese Australians themselves.

Contents

About ChideStudy Press

Purpose
ChideStudy Press is an independent publisher designed to bridge the gap between academic publishers (too expensive and too often located behind firewalls) and popular or trade publishers (too frightened of footnotes and too willing to compromise on content).

Website
https://chidestudypresscom.wordpress.com

Email
chidestudypress@gmail.com

If you don't want to but a copy for yourself
why not recommend that your local library buy one
for you!

www.ingramcontent.com/pod-product-compliance
Lightning Source LLC
Chambersburg PA
CBHW020521030426
42337CB00011B/494